Rudolf Steiner:
his Life and Work

Gilbert Childs was born in 1923 and has spent most of his working life as teacher and education-ist. He became a member of the General Anthro-posophical Society in 1947. He is the author of *Steiner Education* and other books on themes re-lating to spiritual science. He completed his Ph.D. on the evolutionary implications of Steiner's edu-cational theories.

Gilbert Childs

Rudolf Steiner: his Life and Work

Anthroposophic Press

First published in 1995 by Floris Books and
in 1996 by Anthroposophic Press

Published by Anthroposophic Press Inc
RR 4 Box 94A1, Hudson NY 12534

Front cover picture: Rudolf Steiner
Back cover picture: the second Goetheanum, Switzerland

ISBN 0–88010–391–4

Printed in Great Britain

Contents

1. Researching in two worlds

Rudolf Steiner was born on February 27, 1861 in the small town of Kraljevec, then on the border between Austria and Hungary, but now in Croatia. The elder son of a family of three born to Johann Steiner, a stationmaster employed by the South Austrian Railway, and his wife Franziska, his early childhood was that of a typical country boy, happily familiar with the local peasantry and villagers.

His childhood was unremarkable enough, except for the fact that at about the age of seven he became aware of an invisible, intangible world existing in parallel to the ordinary world of the senses open to everyone. He realized that it was futile to speak of his experiences, usual to him but not to his family and others, and so remained silent about them. This silence was to last for thirty-four years.

Personal development

As one who was keenly interested in everything to do with the invisible as well as visible worlds, Steiner made every effort to explore both. Indeed, he was more at home, so to speak, among the phenomena of the supersensory, spiritual worlds — of which he found it almost impossible to speak to anyone — than he was in the everyday material world of sense-perception open to us all. He found learning facts and data concerning natural objects and processes extremely hard. His own words are worth quoting in full here:

Rudolf Steiner

It was always difficult for me to fix in memory such
external data, for instance, as must be assimilated in the
world of science. I had to see a natural object again and
again in order to know what it was called, in what scientific class of objects it was listed, and the like. I might
even say that the sense-world was for me rather shad-
owy, or like a picture. It passed before my mind in
pictures, whereas my bond with the spiritual always bore
the genuine character of reality.[1]

This condition lasted until Steiner was in his mid-thirties, and
it was only then that he felt a genuine equipoise with regard to
both the sensory and the supersensory realms.

At school his performance was initially below average. A
poor speaker, he found writing and spelling very difficult to
master. By contrast, reading came easily to him, and he was
quick to grasp ideas. Of great comfort and significance to him
was a geometry textbook which the assistant teacher had left
lying about. Rudolf quickly realized that the geometrical shapes
filling page after page represented forms which existed independently of the outer world of the senses, but nevertheless were
true realities in the inner world of ideas. With great relief, he
understood that reconciliation between the visible and tangible
world of the senses and the invisible, intangible world of the
spirit was possible. Further confirmation of the co-existence of
these worlds was provided by the rituals and liturgies of the
Roman Catholic Church into which he had been baptized. The
source of his joy and comfort was not merely in the outer religious content of the church services, but in the fact that he
could observe in the supersensory worlds the consequences of
the actions of the celebrant in the material world, and how the
priest acted as mediator between the two.

Johann Steiner had ambitions for his elder son to become a
railway civil engineer, and when the time came for his second-
ary education Rudolf was sent to a technical school, where he
received a thorough grounding in the natural sciences. Even as
a boy he spent his pocket money on second-hand philosophical
books, and when at the age of fourteen he acquired a copy of

Rudolf Steiner in 1869 at the age of 18.

Kant's *Critique of Pure Reason* he tackled it enthusiastically, despite the need to read many pages twenty times or more to master their contents. Though he did not find the help from it that he was seeking, his conviction persisted that only through philosophical method could he find the bridge between the two worlds — the material and the spiritual. This was a bridge he himself would have to construct.

In 1879, the young Steiner matriculated with distinction, and in the autumn commenced advanced studies in mathematics, natural history and chemistry at Vienna Technical College. He had by then decided to become a science teacher, but whilst he was at technical school such were his tenacity and powers of application that he taught himself the usual arts subjects, including Latin and Greek, in which he coached his fellow-students in order to contribute towards his parents' meagre income. Throughout, he continued studying whatever books on philosophy he could lay hands on, and whenever he was able, attended lectures on the subject at the University of Vienna. He took a keen interest in the work of contemporary philosophers,

Karl Julius Schröer.

Rudolf Steiner in Vienna.

particularly Fichte. However he became increasingly aware of the problems involved in reconciling the material and spiritual worlds to the satisfaction of orthodox scientists and thinkers.

Steiner as scholar and teacher

Within the first two weeks at college Rudolf Steiner became acquainted with Karl Julius Schröer, then Professor of German Language and Literature, whose special interests included the works of Goethe and Schiller. However, Steiner was more interested in Goethe's work as a scientist than as a man of letters, and he was intrigued by his work in the field of optics. Through his own studies of Goethe's theory of colour, which contrasts sharply with the Newtonian approach adopted by conventional science, Steiner found further confirmation of the constant interplay between the material and spiritual worlds. As well as following the usual college curriculum he applied himself in his spare time to studies in botany and anatomy from a Goethean standpoint.

In 1883, when Steiner was only twenty-two years old, he was invited by Professor Joseph Kürschner, upon Schröer's recommendation, to edit Goethe's scientific writings for the *Deutsche Nationalliteratur.* Steiner accepted the task enthusiastically, for to him it seemed like a stroke of destiny; and indeed it did pave his way forward. Goethe himself had been deeply disappointed by the fact that his scientific work had passed relatively unnoticed during his lifetime, and Steiner did much to make restitution. He was delighted and greatly encouraged when he came upon Goethe's notion of the 'sensory-supersensory form' which is interposed, both for true natural vision and for spiritual perception, between what the senses grasp and what the spirit apprehends.[2]

Already interested in teaching as a career, Rudolf Steiner was stimulated by Schröer's little book *Problems of Teaching,* which formed the substance of many conversations between the two men. He accepted Schröer's principle that the imparting of knowledge *per se* to children is a means to an end rather than

*Johann
Wolfgang
von Goethe
(1749–1832).*

an end in itself, and only incidental to the development of the entire human being in terms of lifelong learning.

In 1884, again upon the recommendation of Schröer, Rudolf Steiner became tutor to the four sons of Ladislaus and Pauline Specht, a post he held for the following six years. His greatest responsibility was towards the youngest boy, Otto, who was then ten years of age and suffering from a hydrocephalic condition. He was considered to be virtually ineducable, but Steiner took up the challenge with characteristic dedication. He was able to perceive the correlation between the boy's soul-spiritual nature and his bodily nature, and it was then, declared Steiner

Rudolf Steiner in Weimar in 1889.

in later years, that he undertook his 'real course of study in physiology and psychology.' Within two years he had success-fully brought Otto, whose hydrocephalic condition had by then regressed, to grammar school entrance standard, when he continued with his normal education, eventually qualifying as a medical practitioner. There is little doubt that the experience he gained during these years was of paramount importance in enabling Steiner to formulate the new art of education which he implemented some thirty or so years later.

These Vienna years were happy and fruitful ones for him. Ever of a sociable and affable nature, he mixed freely with the local intelligentsia with whom he exchanged ideas. He knew from experience, of course, that he had to choose with great care those who could act as a sounding-board for his more challenging theories. At the same time, he pursued his studies concerning Goethe during this period, his *Theory of Knowledge Implicit in Goethe's World-Conception,* being published in 1886.

Weimar years

The seven years at Weimar, from 1890 to 1897, amounted to something of a trial for Steiner. They contrasted sharply with the happy Vienna days spent among stimulating and convivial company, with friends who provided a warm social atmosphere and with whom he could discuss his budding philosophies. His expectations concerning the Goethe-Schiller Archives in Wei-mar met with disappointment and even disillusionment. Here he felt somewhat unwelcome and spiritually isolated, and was stifled by the dry atmosphere of pedantry and icy intellectual-ism which prevailed. In their approach to Goethe and Schiller, his colleagues were concerned rather with the philological nice-ties of text than with the spirit which had breathed through those authors and their living ideas. However, he found com-pensation in the fact that he was able to meet frequently with distinguished cultural personalities of the day, including Hein-rich von Treitschke, Hermann Grimm, Gabrielle Reuter and

Fritz Koegel. It may be that, in this spiritual desert, he was being left to work out his own ideas with greater clarity. After he obtained his PhD at the University of Rostock in 1891, his Weimar years were punctuated by the publication of book after book, notably his *Philosophy of Freedom* in 1894 and *Goethe's World View* in 1897. These works are central to understanding the philosophical foundations of the spiritual-scientific activities that followed.

During his years at Weimar Steiner reached his thirty-fifth birthday, which marked a great advance in his personal development. In his autobiography, he describes the change which took place within him:

> Whereas before this time ... sense-perception, and especially the retention of this in memory, required the greatest effort on my part, everything now became quite different. An attentiveness ... to the sense-perceptible now awakened in me. Details became more important; I had the feeling that the sense-world had something to reveal which it alone could reveal.[3]

It was at this time that Steiner, so to speak, 'came of age' as a citizen of both spiritual and material worlds. By tenacious effort, he had reached the stage where his reconciliation of sensory and supersensory phenomena could stand up to the philosophical and scientific tests of others.

Berlin

In 1897 Rudolf Steiner was glad to shake off the dust of Weimar, and he moved to Berlin. This next period also lasted some seven years, and was full of incident. As joint editor with Otto Hartleben, a bohemian character whom he found difficult to get along with, he was occupied for three years with *The Literary Magazine.* However, once again he found himself in the company of warm and stimulating people, and on October 30, 1899 married Anna Eunicke, a widow twelve years his

Anna Eunicke, Rudolf Steiner's first wife.

senior, at whose house he had lodged while in Weimar. In the same year he took up a position as teacher at the Workers' Educational Institute in Berlin, one which he held until the end of 1904. His lectures there were well received, and included courses on history, German literature, and the history of science.

It was during the late 1880s, during his happy Vienna years, that Steiner first came into contact with Theosophy, which embodied for the most part arcane teachings of Oriental — mainly Indian — origins. The Theosophical Society, founded in the United States in 1875 by Henry Steel Olcott (1832–1907) and Helena Petrovna Blavatsky (1831–91), held a certain attraction for Steiner, but he was by no means in full agreement with its

Helena Petrova Blavatsky and Henry Steel Olcott.

doctrines and practices. He never took any traditions, esoteric or otherwise, at their face value, but always tested them against his own researches into the spiritual worlds, thus maintaining his rigorous standards as spiritual-scientific investigator.

Many are under the mistaken impression that, because of Steiner's early interest in and association with theosophical teachings, his system of anthroposophy had somehow grown out of these. The case is rather that, before the turn of the century, his association with 'official' theosophy was purely informal. Then, on September 22, 1900, at the invitation of Count and Countess Brockdorff, who were leading members of the Theosophical Society in Berlin, Rudolf Steiner gave a lecture to the local membership about Nietzsche, presumably because earlier in the month he had also given lectures concerning him. A week later, also at the invitation of the Brockdorffs, he gave a further lecture entitled *Goethe's Secret Revelation* in the Theosophical Library. This was his first address ever of a purely esoteric nature, and it was followed a further week later by the first lecture of a series of twenty-seven on mysticism and the mystics of the Middle Ages.

However, Steiner was well aware of the futility of harking back to past ages if the needs of humanity in the twentieth century and beyond were to be effectively addressed. He saw clearly that no kind of modern mysticism, any more than the traditional esoteric teachings that lay at the basis of the Theosophical movement, could lead to the effective solution of the problems facing humankind. A new impulse was abroad in the world, and he took on the responsibility of fostering and developing it, both in ideal and practical terms.

He made it clear from the start that he would not lecture on any subject that he had not thoroughly researched himself, either through orthodox scholarship, or through his own investigations of an esoteric nature.[4] After a long apprenticeship commenced as far back as the late 1880s he had 'arrived' as a speaker on a wide range of cultural and esoteric themes. Important for anthroposophy was October 5, 1902, when Steiner, seasoned, mature and knowledgeable, commenced his course of twenty-five lectures on *Christianity as Mystical Fact,* which appeared in book form in 1902. This proved in many respects to anticipate an important date in 1923, twenty-one years later. This work placed the Christ and his mission squarely into the context of history, addressing both as *fact* rather than matters of belief and tradition, religious or otherwise. Steiner states in his autobiography that the object of his lectures 'was to set forth the evolution from the ancient mysteries to the mystery of Golgotha in such a way as to show that, in this evolution, not merely earthly historical forces but spiritual supramundane influences were at work.'[5]

Steiner's main objections to Theosophical teachings centred around their lack of proper recognition and appreciation of Christ's mission and its purpose, and also for Christianity as a

Annie Besant.

significant impulse in the history of Western civilization. He
made his position perfectly clear, and it therefore came as a
surprise to many people to learn that, on October 20, 1902,
Steiner accepted an invitation to join the Theosophical Society,
agreeing to take up the duties of Secretary-General of its newly
founded German branch. During the same year he attended a

Rudolf Steiner as a teacher, Berlin, 1901.

Theosophical Congress in London where he made the acquain-
tance of Annie Besant, who was Secretary-General of the
Society's British section. Also attending the conference was
Marie von Sivers, whom Steiner had first met when she attended one of his Berlin lectures on mysticism. It marked a
stroke of destiny, as events were to show.

Time to go public

In the period around the turn of the century Rudolf Steiner was
faced with a dilemma: should he remain silent about his investigations and findings, or go public with them? He knew that this
would be far from easy. Moreover, his life to date was a story
of inner loneliness, of perpetual struggle to build a bridge between the material and spiritual worlds. He found it necessary,
though difficult, to describe supersensory beings and events in
words already formulated to express experiences, concepts and
ideas almost entirely derived from sense-impressions proper to
the material world familar to us all.

On October 8, 1902, in a lecture to the Giordano Bruno
Union, Steiner declared his life's aim to be the founding of new
methods of spiritual research on a scientific basis. He was then
forty-one years old. Not surprisingly, the unfamiliar manner of
his researches and the unorthodox character of his findings met
with strong opposition, even extending to attempts on his life.
The probable reason for this antagonism is the widespread sus-
picion that is usually attached to anything even slightly associated with 'the occult'; and it may partly have been due also to
the apparent transformation in Steiner's behaviour and standing
as respectable philosopher, scientist and scholar, into someone
who seemingly talked nonsense and was no longer worth taking
seriously. Contemporaries who took this view could have had
no idea of the risks involved and the tremendous courage
needed for Steiner to take this irreversible step.

As time went on, whilst Steiner was giving lectures on such

Marie von Sivers in 1901.

diverse topics as religion, education, social issues, history, human nature and so on with all the authority of a specialist in these fields, many former sympathizers deserted him. They did not appreciate that he exemplified a new type of Universal Man, whose expertise was not confined to the fragmented speciality, the conventional, the orthodox. Here was one who was capable of perceiving not only the materially manifest world, but also the *occult,* in the true sense of what is hidden and unmanifest. Our bodily senses, themselves composed of matter, are capable only of perceiving material objects; for spiritual perception we need to develop *supersensory* organs. Steiner was an explorer of worlds closed to the ordinary powers of sense-perception, and few were capable of following him. He was wise enough to show the way, long and arduous as it undoubtedly is, to those who wished to acquire supersensory knowledge for themselves, and this period was punctuated with such revelatory books as *Knowledge of the Higher Worlds and its Attainment, Reincarnation and Karma, Stages of Higher Knowledge,* and *Occult Science.*

In Steiner's writings, the faculty of exact perception into the spiritual worlds has little in common with what is generally understood by *clairvoyance,* a word that carries with it unfortunate connotations of unreliability and even charlatanry. Steiner, trained as a scientist and dedicated to the investigative standards of scientific research, strove constantly to apply a corresponding rigour to his own investigations. The results of these could be verified by anyone whose powers of perception were comparable with his, and also by those who applied ordinary powers of observation and logic to his findings. Mainly for this reason he felt justified in referring to himself as a 'spiritual researcher' and the body of knowledge thus accumulated as a genuine 'spiritual science' *(Geisteswissenschaft).* He used 'anthroposophy' as an alternative term for this.

By January 1905 Rudolf Steiner's depth of knowledge concerning both the material and immaterial worlds had ensured his success as a lecturer, and invitations for him to speak poured in. His life's work had begun.

2. From Theosophy to anthroposophy

Early initiatives

From the moment that the German Section of the Theosophical Society was founded in 1902, Rudolf Steiner realized that, if his anthroposophical work was to be carried on under its patronage, a channel of communication to the general public would be essential. With the help and encouragement of Marie von Sivers, he founded the monthly journal *Luzifer,* which was launched in 1903. This name was of the greatest significance for the future. Steiner had in mind an axiom found in the ancient mysteries: *Christus verus Luciferus* — 'Christ is the true Lucifer [Light-bearer]'; for what he later often came to refer to as the 'Christ Event' was to figure large in the development of anthroposophy. The number of subscribers increased rapidly, and it was not long before the Vienna journal *Gnosis* was taken over, and the magazine was renamed *Lucifer-Gnosis.* Steiner himself wrote most of the copy, and Marie von Sivers dealt with the correspondence. The numbers of subscribers increased steadily, but in 1908 it ceased publication — not for lack of subscribers, but because of other growing pressures, mainly on time.

During this first period of his public work, Steiner's lectures gave indications of future practical applications of anthroposophy, particularly in the areas of the arts, medicine, education, and biblical and other wisdom literature. In Berlin in 1907 he gave for the first time a lecture *The Education of the Child in the Light of Anthroposophy* which was delivered in many other cities also. In this manner, as in the case of other initiatives that were to flourish only much later, he sowed the seeds that ger-

minated and grew. Other lectures dealt with the human constitution from the standpoint of spiritual science, health and illness,
reincarnation and karma, historical personalities and events, the
spiritual hierarchies, elemental beings, and many other topics.

Years later, he mentioned that at this time the beings and
events of the spiritual world 'drew near' to him, facilitating his
efforts. For the most part it was a matter of addressing those
people who had ears to hear, who felt themselves drawn to a
new phenomenon — an actual science of the spirit — and
wished to learn more. During those early years most of
Steiner's lectures were given to comparatively small audiences,
comprising enthusiastic members of the Theosophical Society.
At that time he had no intention that his lecture cycles be
published, for he invariably tailored content and style of presentation to his audience. For this reason, a certain mastery — and
indeed acceptance — of his premises and terminology is necessary to make much sense of many of his printed lecture cycles.
His public lectures, which accounted for a comparatively small
percentage of the six thousand and more that he delivered during his career, assumed no knowledge of anthroposophy, and
are immediately understandable.

By contrast, his written books are not always easy to com-
prehend. His somewhat convoluted literary style was deliberately adopted for several reasons. The most important of these,
perhaps, was that he was uncompromising in his aim to make
as clear as possible to his readers what was clear to him, bear-
ing in mind the difficulties of attempting to describe the beings
and events of an immaterial world in language best suited to
depicting the material world. However, he never gave in to the
temptation to 'devalue' spiritual science by oversimplifying its
more abstruse features, as he knew that this would almost certainly lead to misunderstanding and error.

Steiner deliberately shaped the style, approach and treatment
of his literary material so as to lead the reader through a genuine spiritual exercise. The word *difficult* was never part of his
vocabulary; he held the view that nothing of value ever comes

Rudolf Steiner in 1905.

easily to anyone, and that the possession of initiative and the capacity for hard work should be taken for granted. Himself indefatigable, he was demanding of others. During lecture tours, conferences and suchlike there were always queues of people — the curious, the interested, the time-wasters — outside the door of his hotel room, and his was invariably the last light to be put out, usually in the early hours. Yet he was always bright and active the following day, his customarily affable, amenable and approachable self.

Steiner loved people, and had an impish sense of humour that all the known photographs of him seem to deny, as there his features are always grave and serious. In a letter to Anthroposophical Society members from his deathbed, he makes this observation:

> Gravity in the face of any being is the reflection of the cosmos in that being; a smiling countenance is the expression of that which shines forth from the being itself into the world.[6]

This attitude is certainly revealed in his own gravity of mien in known photographs. It is almost as if allowing himself to be portrayed smiling in public might suggest that in his work he was expressing a purely personal element.

This early period saw the publication of Steiner's basic books. In later years, when asked which publications he would recommend for serious enquirers and beginners, he gave these as *Theosophy* (1904), *Knowledge of the Higher Worlds and its Attainment* (1904), *Occult Science* (1909), *The Spiritual Guidance of the Individual and Humanity* (1911), and *West and East — Contrasting Worlds* (1922). Of *Occult Science* (1909), he declared that every other written work and lecture course could be interleaved between its pages. He made a similar statement concerning his four mystery Plays (1910–13): that they contained the essence of the whole of anthroposophy in artistic form.

East and West — an unhappy alliance

On his own admission, Rudolf Steiner saw as his main aim in those crucial first years, from 1902 to 1909, as not only to develop and disseminate anthroposophy, but also to bring the doctrines of the Theosophical Society 'into contrast with the spirituality of occidental civilization with its middle point in the mystery of Golgotha.'[7] This necessarily involved making known his strikingly original Christology, which is undoubtedly the central pillar of his whole spiritual-scientific edifice.

He approached the enigma of the Incarnation purely and solely from his standpoint as spiritual researcher, free from any historical, scriptural or doctrinal bias. Regarding, as he did, Christ's mission as pivotal in cosmic and earthly history, the fact that the Incarnation and the momentous life-events of Jesus Christ became the basis of religious belief was strictly speaking, for Steiner, beside the point.

As documents widely taken to chronicle the 'Christ Event,' the Scriptures not unnaturally came under his scrutiny, and here he relied on a fuller and deeper understanding of the biblical texts through his own spiritual insights. His lecture courses on topics such as the Creation and the Apocalypse comment illuminatingly on the symbolical and metaphorical language employed in scriptural writing.

According to their own standpoint, people's reactions to these commentaries ranged from total incredulity through antagonism to relief and satisfaction. As ever, Steiner never attempted to persuade or influence, entice or convert; he always set out notions based on his findings, and left it to individuals to make of them what they could according to their lights. He was a passionate believer in the rights to freedom of everyone, for how each of us exercises them is our own reponsibility. His book *Christianity as Mystical Fact* served as a general background to the lectures he gave later, particularly after relinquishing his position as lecturer at the Working Men's College in Berlin in December 1904.

Books on spiritual training and esoteric matters, as well as

Rudolf Steiner with Annie Besant.

lectures dealing with Rosicrucianism, the fundamentals of 'popular occultism' and suchlike paved the way for courses which gradually became more and more revelatory. These included lectures on John's Gospel from 1906–9 (five courses), on that of Luke (1900), Matthew (1910) and Mark (1910 and 1912); *From Jesus to Christ* (1910) and *The Fifth Gospel* (1913).

At the Budapest Conference in the summer of 1909 Rudolf Steiner declared that the mission of Christ to the earth was an event unique in cosmic and human history. In his address *From Buddha to Christ,* he contended that the Christ could not in any way be compared with other great leaders of mankind; that these were only forerunners and preparers of the way for the Incarnation and subsequent fulfilment of his task. During a conversation with Annie Besant, Steiner warned her that they had, in effect, reached the parting of the ways. In 1910 he told her: 'A Theosophy which lacks the means of grasping Christianity is entirely valueless for the culture of the present day.'[8] At the General Meeting of the German Section of the Theosophical Society on October 24, 1909, he gave four lectures which made direct reference to *anthroposophy,* drawing members' attention to the event which marked the foundation of the Section in 1902, seven years earlier.

The Krishnamurti scandal

The actual break with the Theosophical Society did not come until 1913, and this was inevitable in the face of the events which led up to it. In 1909, whilst at the headquarters of the Theosophical Society in Adyar in India, leading theosophist the Rev Charles Leadbeater spotted two boys, Jiddu Krishnamurti and his younger brother Nityananda bathing in the river. He made the 'discovery' that the older boy was none other than the 'Vehicle of the New World Teacher, the Lord Matraiya,' whose last incarnation had been in the person of Jesus Christ.[9] Leadbeater convinced Annie Besant, then President of the Theosophical Society, of this, and after prolonged battles in and

out of court, she was apppointed guardian of Krishnamurti,
whom she sent to England to be educated, together with Nityananda for company, in 1911. By then the Order of the Star in
the East had been formed, Mrs Besant and Leadbeater anticipat-
ing that it would take twenty years or so to prepare Krishnamurti to reach the necessary degree of perfection for his
'Christly' mission. However, although Krishnamurti did turn out
to be a sensitive poet and deep thinker, on August 3, 1929,
during a summer camp at Ommen in Holland, he announced the
dissolution of the Order of the Star. Echoing in a strange way
Rudolf Steiner's own passionate belief in freedom was Krishnamurti's closing declaration: 'My only concern is to set men
absolutely, unconditionally free.'[10] He died in 1986 at the age
of ninety-one.

Christ in the world

Steiner went on to develop what he had hinted at much earlier
(1901–2) in a course of lectures published soon after as *Christianity as Mystical Fact.* Here he maintained that his whole
Christology was conceived and developed directly out of his
perception of the spiritual worlds, without reference to traditional scriptures or any other external authority.

That Christianity has evolved into organized religion with its
established doctrines and dogmas, various sectarian beliefs and
so on is not of course the fault of the Scriptures themselves; it
is rather due to misunderstanding and misinterpretation, not to
mention poor translation. Even deliberate angling of translations
and meanings in favour of a certain point of view, is not un-
known. As with every other religion or system of belief rather
than direct knowledge, there are *esoteric* as well as *exoteric*
aspects of Christianity: the former long kept hidden by a select
and literally ordained few from the general masses, whose understanding of them was considered to be limited. For popular
consumption, a fare of sermonizing, together with dramatized
biblical teachings in the form of mystery plays, cautionary tales
and suchlike, was considered sufficient.

Christ, the central figure of the Group by Rudolf Steiner.

Briefly, Rudolf Steiner sought to show that the exalted spiritual being, which came to be designated the Christ, was none other than the Sun-Being (the Light of the World) that had been worshipped in previous ages in the mystery centres of the Persians, Egyptians and Greeks, and in more recent times the Teutonic, Norse, Celtic and other pagan cultures previous to his descent to earth. At the Baptism by John in the River Jordan, the Christ Being 'descended,' that is to say incarnated into, the bodily vehicle of Jesus of Nazareth, therein to dwell until his crucifixion. Since the Resurrection he has remained on our planet, present but unseen to all but those with supersensory perception: 'I am with you always, even unto the end of the age.' (Matt.28:20) Christ, the Being of Light and Love, was fully aware of the purposes of his mission: 'For I know whence I come and whither I go ...' (John 8:14).

Steiner maintained that it was possible for the Christ to be *incarnated,* that is, descend into an earthly vehicle, *once* and once only. In his writings and lectures refuting the absurdities of Annie Besant's claims concerning Krishnamurti, Steiner averred that Christ was indeed to 'come again,' not in a material body but in a supersensory fashion which, moreover, would be perceptible to those who earnestly and patiently underwent the requisite spiritual training. Those able to perceive the 'etheric' Christ would have a similar experience to that undergone by Paul whilst on the road to Damascus. Paul recognized *the Christ* as a purely spiritual being; he never knew Christ when still incarnated in the physical body of Jesus of Nazareth.

Steiner went so far as to state that it was part of the mission of anthroposophy to prepare the way for a true Christianity that would be self-validating through personal experience. He maintained that in course of time more and more people would become capable of apprehending the Christ — as a spiritual being — for themselves. Scriptures and other written records would eventually become redundant as a source for sustaining belief, as this would give way to directly acquired *knowledge.* The two factors essential for the future development of humankind are: bringing to wider consciousness the knowledge that the human being is essentially *spiritual* in nature, and as such has spiritual needs; and the process of reunification of religion, art and science. It is the current imbalance towards materialism, which also serves to isolate science from our other fields of knowledge, which is responsible for the manifold problems of the twentieth century.

3. Art and human nature

During the period from 1909 to 1916, the development of anthroposophy principally involved the artistically-creative areas. In 1906 Steiner met Edouard Schuré, whose mystery drama *The Sacred Drama of Eleusis* was performed in the Concert Hall in Munich, on the occasion of a Congress of the Federation of European Sections of the Theosophical Society during May 1907. For the first time, an *artistic* element had been introduced into the usual Congress programme, for much to Rudolf Steiner's disappointment and regret, art played little part within the Society. Original productions of Edouard Schuré's mystery plays *The Sacred Drama of Eleusis* and *The Children of Lucifer* were performed during the Theosophical Society's Congress in the Concert Hall in Munich in 1907 and 1909 respectively, and were much appreciated.

Rudolf Steiner's first wife died on March 19, 1911, and three years later Steiner married Marie von Sivers. She had trained professionally at drama schools in St Petersburg and Paris, and her voice was rich and melodious. Her gifts in this respect led to her developing an art of recitation and declamation which was taken up in the dramatic productions which were to follow. She translated Edouard Schuré's drama *The Children of Lucifer* and Rudolf Steiner edited it for stage production in 1909, also in Munich. Its performance at the Congress there by members of the Munich Group, thus established the custom, still observed, that artistic activities be included as part of all future anthroposophical congresses and conferences. Steiner maintained that artistic representation of a philosophy such as anthroposophy is richer in terms of spirituality, and a

Edouard Schuré.

Performers of the first mystery play.

more powerful 'awakener' than any rationalistic, intellectualistic presentation of it. Accordingly, his own mystery plays were performed on the occasion of future Munich Congresses: *The Portal of Initiation* (1910 and 1911); *The Soul's Probation* (1911 and 1912); *The Guardian of the Threshold* (1912 and 1913), and *The Soul's Awakening* (1913). The outbreak of the First World War in August 1914 put an end to further plans.

A new art of movement

In 1913 the very first eurythmy performance was staged. This new and original art of movement was formulated by Rudolf

Eurythmy performed by some of the original eurythmists.

Steiner from indications gained from the spiritual worlds, and was developed in co-operation with Marie von Sivers and others over several years. When we speak or sing, we create patterned forms and gestures with our breath and resulting sound, and it is these forms which furnish the source of the whole art of eurythmy. This why Steiner often referred to it as 'visible speech' and 'visible song.' The report in Genesis that God *spoke* in order to bring things into existence is echoed in the use of the creative *Word* in John's Gospel. 'God did eurythmy' said Steiner, 'and in doing so created the human form.' He once characterized eurythmy as 'soul gymnastics,' and only those with experience of doing eurythmy themselves can appreciate this.

As an art in its own right, eurythmy has nothing in common with mime or any kind of dance, traditional or contrived. Performers of *speech eurythmy* carry out arm and hand gestures which correspond to the sounds of the vowels and consonants occurring in the 'speech' element, at the same time tracing artistically conceived footwork patterns, known as 'forms,' on the stage platform. These may range from the fairly simple to the extremely intricate, but are carried out with grace and beauty.

In *tone eurythmy,* the appropriate limb movements correspond with the melodies and rhythms of the music being played, but the principles are those of speech eurythmy. Performers may be male or female, working either solo or in groups, depending on the size of stage, the drama or text being recited, or the music being played. They are dressed in long, loose, flowing garments of colours considered to bring the 'gestures' of the word-sounds to life visually, and diaphanous silk veils, also of varying colours intended to convey the prevailing mood of the piece being performed.

Steiner wished eurythmy to be the only compulsory lesson for children of Waldorf schools. Its importance in terms of the overall curriculum, pedagogy and didactics is undoubtedly enormous, and this can perhaps be fully appreciated only by those who have studied both eurythmy and Steiner/Waldorf educational principles. Eventually, too, a system of *curative eurythmy* was developed by Steiner in collaboration with medically qualified colleagues, and this has been demonstrated to be a valuable extension of the art of healing.

From the moment of its inception, Marie von Sivers took the greatest possible interest in eurythmy, and she was largely responsible for its further implementation whilst working in close collaboration with Rudolf Steiner. Classes for beginners in eurythmy are now held in a number of centres and professional eurythmists regularly perform throughout the world. However, eurythmy has not met with widespread recognition and appreciation except in the educational and therapeutic circles which run on Steiner principles.

In the artistic sphere, Steiner's ideas on architecture and the

Rudolf Steiner and Marie von Sivers in Stuttgart in 1908.

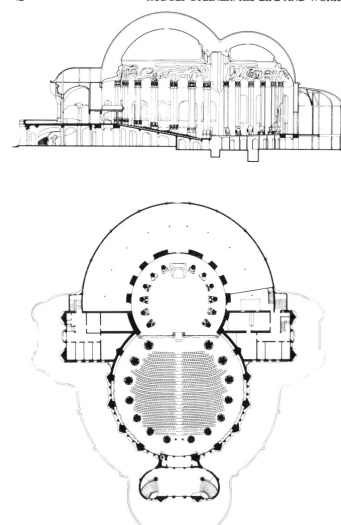

First Goetheanum plan and section.

plastic arts in general have been developed more widely. Here he drew to a great extent on the principle of metamorphosis in an 'organic' style. His ideas on the development of the visual arts included various innovative ways of using colour and black and white drawing.

The first Goetheanum

The growing need for some kind of building which would serve as a lecture hall as well as providing facilities necessary for the dramatic productions and eurythmy soon became apparent. Plans and efforts to establish such a building in Munich failed, but in September 1912 came the offer of a building site at Dornach, a village near Basel in Switzerland, which Rudolf Steiner gratefully accepted. In the same month the decision was taken to form the Anthroposophical Society, and to sever all links with the Theosophical Society. This was made complete and formal in January 1913. These decisions were momentous ones for Steiner and his associates in view of the two calamitous wars that were to follow, during which Switzerland's neutrality was preserved. Hitherto the more intellectual and scientific activities had been concentrated in Berlin, notably at the Architektenhaus, and the artistic activities at the Philharmonic Hall in Munich; and these formed a kind of polarity.

Now came the opportunity to unite them in a single location. Steiner himself undertook the task of designing the building, and instead of drawing plans he constructed a sizeable model. Accordingly, the foundation 'stone' of the first Goetheanum, which in fact consisted of two interpenetrating dodecahedrons made of copper, was laid on September 20, 1913, and it remained in the same spot to serve the same function for the second Goetheanum, which was built later on the same site. Rudolf Steiner took up residence in Dornach on April 1, 1914, and on the same day, the roof of the Goetheanum now fully in place, the 'topping-out' ceremony was celebrated. But the real work of turning it into the truly wonderful work of art as well as architecture that it was, could only then begin.

Rudolf Steiner and Marie von Sivers were married on December 24, 1914, but work went on as usual. It carried on during the years of the First World War: the construction workers, carvers, artists and painters, drawn from no fewer than seventeen countries, could hear the rumbling of gunfire in nearby Alsace. The outbreak of war, foreseen as inevitable by Steiner and many other contemporary thinkers, was an occasion of much sorrow and distress to him. The spiritual causes lying behind the material events were, moreover, abundantly clear to him.

Since the impulse to construct a building that would facilitate progress in both the arts and the sciences from spiritual-scientific bases, it was considered that the new Goetheanum building should incorporate this duality in an artistic way. Accordingly it was designed by Rudolf Steiner, as a construction of two intersecting cylinders, one smaller than the other, capped by hemispherical domes roofed in Norwegian slate, with sufficient space to accommodate audiences of a thousand people. The grey-green slates, which were used on the Glass House and other buildings, glittered on sunny days and glistened on wet days. The building was constructed entirely of seven different woods, namely ash, oak, elm, hornbeam, cherry, maple and birch, the whole structure standing on a concrete plinth. The result, in many ways reminiscent of a violin, was a colossal work of art. Its wooden walls were richly adorned with carvings, and the wooden pillars with their capitals and bases, and the architraves, door and window frames were also carved to ornate designs. In order to achieve sufficiently large blocks of wood suitable for carving, thick planks were glued together, and this so firmly as to withstand the heavy blows of mallet on chisel.

The outstanding characteristic of the interior décor was the principle of *metamorphosis* which was everywhere evident. This principle, continuously at work in the spiritual worlds and in the living processes of nature, here furnished a perpetual reminder of the work so ardently researched by Goethe, after whom the edifice was named. Stained-glass windows, etched and ground so as to form radiant light-pictures, and paintings on the roofs of both cupolas, added to the overwhelming impression and

Rudolf Steiner with a model of the first Goetheanum in 1914.

Rudolf Steiner working in his studio in 1919.

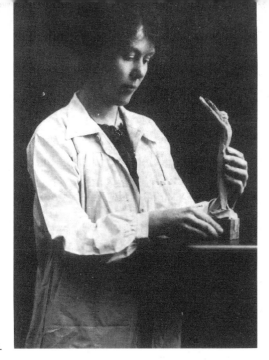

Edith Maryon.

invitation to aesthetic enjoyment. The whole building was designed as an entirely appropriate setting for artistic activities in the shape of music, drama and eurythmy as well as for the spoken word, the rostrum being situated at the point of intersection between the two domes and exactly over the foundation 'stone.' The exterior was similarly inviting, and the overall intention was that no building should be more evocative of spirit at work in matter. In this case, the spirit had been implanted in the medium of wood by the devoted work of considerable numbers of wood-carvers drawn from many nations.

Perhaps the most striking feature, which was for the most part the work of Rudolf Steiner himself, assisted by the English sculptor Edith Maryon, was a mighty wooden sculpture that has come to be known as the 'Group.' Its original name as given by Rudolf Steiner is *Representative of Man with Ahriman and Lucifer*. However, later he accepted the interpretation that the central figure was representative rather of the Christ. It is seen to be holding at bay — or rather in balance — Lucifer as Tempter, whose aim it is to convince us that we are ourselves gods; and of Ahriman, as Satan, who seeks to persuade us that we are mechanical creations consisting of matter only. The philosophical rationale underpinning Steiner's ideas is impossible to summarize in a few words; but it could be said that Lucifer would have us all accept *spiritualism,* the doctrine that nothing is real except soul and spirit, and that Ahriman represents *materialism,* that which maintains that nothing is real except matter, and that soul-spiritual phenomena are merely emanations that arise from it. Put yet another way: Lucifer would whirl us away into a world where *feeling* rules, whereas Ahriman would have us believe that *reason* alone should prevail.

Standing some nine and a half metres high, this huge work of art was to have stood in the alcove formed by two pillars standing at the back of the stage in the smaller cupola, but this was never to be; in fact, it was never finished. When the first Goetheanum was burnt down on the night of New Year's Eve, 1921–22, it was still standing, in its uncompleted state, in a carpenter's shop which served as Steiner's studio. Thus it escaped the blaze that, as a result of arson, reduced the once splendid building to ashes, with only the concrete plinth remaining. The statue now stands in a room in the second Goetheanum specially designed to take it.

Steiner withstood this devastating blow to his hopes and endeavours with characteristic stoicism. During the night, as he walked around the building, he was heard to say: 'Much work and long years.' He announced that the New Year's Day programme would go forward as planned, and gave instructions for the carpenter's shop to be made ready. He told his collaborators that it was their 'inner duty' to carry on their work in whatever places were left to them.

Rudolf Steiner maintained that, precisely at the time in history when the human being was regarded as consisting of physical

The Group.

substance only, according to empirical science, the spiritual world was at its most accessible. Western civilization had reached the point when the human soul-faculties of thinking, feeling and willing were presumed to originate in the brain. He stated again and again that it was the mission of anthroposophy to provide the spiritual insights necessary for a more balanced view of nature; otherwise, if the old materialistic way of thinking persisted, with its emphasis on seeking to solve problems by means of the intellect alone, further catastrophes were bound to follow. He had hoped that the Goetheanum building would help to stimulate and enliven people's thinking by virtue of its artistic principle of metamorphosis.

The principle of threefolding

One of Rudolf Steiner's most important breakthroughs came with his announcement of his findings concerning the threefold nature of man and of society. In his book *The Riddle of Man,* published in 1917, Steiner placed on record the results of systematic spiritual research, extending over a period of thirty years, concerning the physical and soul-spiritual components of the human being. In it he contended that the body as a whole, and not merely the nervous activity impounded in it, is the physical basis for psychic life. That is to say, he saw our bodily organization as being threefold: the system of nerves and senses, located mainly in the head, serves our thinking processes; the rhythmic system, comprising heart and lungs, serves our feeling processes, and our metabolic and limbs system, comprising the digestive organs, legs and arms, serves our willing processes.

However, it should be understood that what Steiner meant by *thinking, feeling* and *willing* bears only faint resemblance to how these terms were construed in the pre-scientific natural philosophy of his day, or even to the cognitive, affective and conative (or psycho-motor) attributes recognized by modern psychology.[11] To him they were *functions* of the human soul rather than mere *attributes* of it. Few modern scientists would

concede that we actually have a soul, much less that the actual
seat of our life of feeling is located in our chest, or that our
will-impulses proceed from our digestive system and limbs.
Steiner did not offer 'proof' in anatomical, physiological or
neurological concepts which had been arrived at empirically; he
rather adopted his usual phenomenological-symptomatological
approach, as this accords with his method of regarding nature
artistically as well as scientifically. He argued that both
approaches are equally valid and complement each other. What
appears in science as the Idea is in art the Image, and the
surmounting of the sensory and material by the supersensory
and spiritual is the goal of both art and science. These two
areas of human striving should — and in fact do — complement each other: there are no inconsistencies between them.

Having characterized the threefold bodily nature and paral-
leled it with a threefold soul nature, Steiner also saw the spirit
as threefold, in terms of consciousness: waking, dreaming and
sleeping. Thus as adults we are awake in our thinking (cerebro-
spinal or nervous system); dreaming in our feelings (rhythmic
or heart/lungs system), and asleep in our willing (metabolic/
limbs system). This particular conception of the human being
as a threefold organism, each member of which is itself threefold, is a very fruitful one,

Here in tabular form is Steiner's view of the human constitution in terms of body, soul and spirit in the context of explana-
tions already given:

	Physical expression	Psychological expression	Spiritual expression
Spirit	Nerves/senses	Thinking	Waking
Soul	Heart/lungs	Feeling	Dreaming
Body	Metabolic/ limb system	Willing	Sleeping

This arrangement matches our everyday experience. Obviously, we are fully conscious in our thinking, which is served to a great extent by our nervous system and brain. The heart is the traditional seat of the emotions, and our breathing is also affected by our feelings, which are essentially dreamlike, and we are not capable of controlling them in a fully conscious way. We are 'asleep' in our metabolic system because we are totally unconscious of what is occurring in our digestive system — unless something is wrong. Similarly, we become conscious of any limb or other psycho-motor activity *after* it has been carried out; of the process itself we are totally unconscious.

It might be said accusingly that Steiner was obsessed with this notion of threefolding, seeing trinitarianism everywhere, from a threefold person to a threefold state. This would be treating his ideas superficially, however, and that is why it is so important to make the effort to understand his terminology and to struggle with the apparent strangeness of his ideas.

4. A new social order

The seven-year period from 1917 to the end of 1923 marks the third stage in Steiner's development of anthroposophy. The emphasis was on putting spiritual-scientific principles and knowledge to practical use in many areas of human life and endeavour.

The threefold social order

Steiner contended that the First World War occurred as the result of faulty education, for to him it was clear that if merely intellectual methods of teaching were carried on, the outlook was grim, with more conflicts to follow. He knew that there would be social upheavals and general unrest, with people wishing for change. As human beings are threefold in nature, so this same threefolding should be evident in the life of society, in the spheres of economics, politics and civil rights. The modern state seeks to keep these three firmly under its influence and direction, and this constant disruption and intervention by the state leads only to continuing turmoil and conflict. It is rare for a government ever to 'get it right,' for the state, conceived as a kind of unitary colossus, composed of disparate fragments and functions with their innumerable variables and bureaucratic procedures, is far too unwieldy in operation.

Steiner's solution to the problem was to establish three independently structured, autonomous 'states' within the state, representing the economic, the political and the cultural spheres. Each 'state' should be free to negotiate with respect to its own interests with the other two, and out of this freedom, ideally,

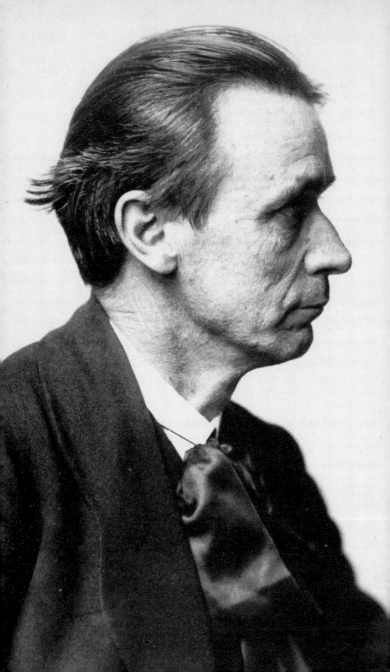

grow mutual regard and common aims, thus contributing to a truly organic rather than a mechanical unity. He claimed that such a threefolding of the body social, and the exercise of freedom involved in its integrating and running procedures, lies as a kind of historical necessity, an inevitable future development.[12] This must and will come, if not by peaceful negotiation and mediation, then by social upheaval and violent change.

By 1917, mounting anger, dissatisfaction and disillusionment which resulted in strikes and social unrest in Germany were but premonitions of what was to follow, and solutions to this social chaos were being earnestly sought. Chaos in Russia following the Revolution added to the sense of urgency. In July of that year Rudolf Steiner was approached for advice concerning such social problems by both Count Otto Lerchenfeld, of the State Council for Bavaria, and Count Ludwig Polzer-Hoditz, brother of the then Prime Minister of Austria. To both men he explained his ideas concerning the necessity of regarding the state as a trinity and not as a unity if social health was to be enjoyed, and both accepted his ideas as practical and reasonable. However, they also considered that there would be difficulties in persuading the general public also to accept them, and they were set aside. A similar reaction came from Prince Max von Baden, who took over as Chancellor of the German Reich in October 1918; he, too, would not take the risk of introducing such revolutionary ideas.[13] Admittedly, it would have required enormous courage, and this was quite understandably lacking. The collapse of established order in Germany in 1918 was inevitable. Mutinies in the ranks of the military services added to the mounting tension; hunger was rife, and law and order in danger of collapse. Hopes and expectations of widely differing sorts were roused on all sides, but the opportunity to remodel German society and political life in a new international framework was missed.

During the first half of 1919, Steiner was very active indeed in his attempts to present to the public the fundamental ideas of the threefold society. To his followers he gave the occult and

Rudolf Steiner in 1916.

The first Goetheanum.

esoteric reasons for inroducing them, confining himself largely
to exoteric aspects when lecturing to trade unionists and work-
men in the factories in and around Stuttgart and other cities. He
and his close collaborators were much in demand for giving
such lectures, not particularly because they were based on anthroposophical spiritual science but because any new idea was
seized upon by the disillusioned public. Discussions with leading industrialists were also held, for they too were anxious to
examine new approaches to their own manifold problems.

In the early spring of 1919, Steiner drew up his thoughts on
the threefolding of society in concise form in a pamphlet entitled *A Call to the German People and the Civilized World!*

and this was distributed widely. In April his book *Towards Social Renewal* was published, which within a year had run to eighty thousand copies. In May 1919 the 'Union for the Threefold Social Order' was founded in Stuttgart, but it was short-lived, for with the acceptance of the Federal Constitution of the Weimar Republic on July 31, 1919 it had become clear that further labours in this field would be fruitless, and the initiative was abandoned. Discouraged, perhaps, but undeterred, Steiner continued tirelessly to give lecture courses on social and pedagogical questions, and by midsummer plans for the setting up of a school for the employees of the Waldorf-Astoria cigarette factory in Stuttgart were well advanced. He saw the situation in Europe in 1919 as not only serious for Germany but also for the rest of the continent, and he went on lecturing as intensively as ever. He perceived the important historical task of awakening people to their true worth as spiritual beings, setting forth ideas which would prevent societies from disintegrating, and giving foundations for a new social fabric for the changed conditions of the times.[14] The impulse provided by the threefold social order is still very much alive in anthroposophical circles, but, as ever, summoning the necessary courage for its implementation is a major factor in limiting its influence.

A portent realized

Rudolf Steiner was convinced that much social unrest, and particularly the feelings of inferiority widespread among the working classes, was not due, as popularly supposed, to frustration in political and economic matters, but to cultural deprivation. He deeply deplored the fact that millions of fourteen-year-old children in the industrial countries of Europe were obliged to discontinue the real process of cultural development and were thrust into the turmoil of industrial and commercial life. The only remedy for this, he asserted, was the participation in free spiritual life, with full allowance for each citizen to be given the best chances for individual development. Furthermore, he was equally convinced that the main problem of education was primarily that of the training of teachers, and that a clear appreciation of the threefold structure of the human being and of the life-epochs that marked development through life, would constitute a sound foundation for a pedagogy based upon the actual nature of the growing child and not on abstract, intellectually conceived theories.

This new approach to the problem of education as a whole implicit in his ideas concerning the causes of social disarray was bound to attract attention. He was approached by Dr Emil Molt, the Managing Director of the Waldorf-Astoria cigarette factory in Stuttgart and a man of vision and compassion, to direct a school for the children of his employees. Rudolf Steiner accepted the invitation immediately. He had, of course, a sound knowledge and experience of educational matters, and it is more than probable that words he had uttered some twelve years earlier arose in his memory. In the lecture *The Education of the Child* which proved popular in the years 1907–9, and was later published in booklet form, he had said: 'Anthroposophical science, *when called upon to build up an art of education,* will be able to indicate all these things in detail ...' [my italics] In April 1919 a preliminary meeting was held, and on September 7, the first Waldorf School opened its doors. Steiner dropped hints about 'a new worldwide order in education,'[15] and he must have known even then that the Waldorf/Steiner schools initiative would eventually be recognized as somehow 'right' for our times, and would become the international movement that it is now. The number of schools worldwide is well over six hundred, and constantly growing.

Steiner education — a thumbnail sketch

Conventional education, with its excessively intellectual approach, 'produces' school leavers who are *unfree,* and this is leading to catastrophes of its own. Steiner envisaged the main task of Waldorf education as being that of providing the appropriate circumstances for human beings to attain to the optimal degree of true freedom which would enable them to

Emil Molt.

fulfil themselves without interfering with the freedom of others. His own philosophy, that of 'ethical individualism,' sets out the principle of *freedom* as absolutely paramount. The main aim of Waldorf education is to 'produce' people whose willing and feeling as well as thinking make them capable of using their powers of individual freedom in supremely practical ways, including the implementation of such ideas as are inherent in the threefold social order. During Steiner's time and since, scholars and others who have appraised his ideas invariably recognize their potential for the social good. He went so far as to predict that its principles, which he had learned from his spiritual-scientific researches would eventually be adopted, probably in desperation as a last resort, by countries or groups of states which had become ungovernable by reason of total social collapse. And it must be said that the signs are ominous.

During the summer of 1919 Steiner invited those whom he considered as possessing the right qualities and potential as teachers in the new school, regardless of previous vocation. He held a 'crash course' for them from August 21 to September 6. He spoke of the Waldorf School as 'a true child of care,' and there is no doubt that it occupied a very special place in his affections as well as his life. He gave it the name *Freie Waldorfschule* in order to make plain his earnest wish and intention that it should be genuinely *frei* in the sense of being *independent,* unconstrained by any kind of outside authority, particularly that of the state.*

During the early years he was obliged to make compromises with the Württemberg educational boards, but once established, the Stuttgart school became entirely independent. It was typical of him that he concerned himself with the day-to-day problems of running the school, and none was too small that he would not give his attention to it if requested. He abhorred any kind of interference from outside bodies, emphasising that schools should be run by the teachers themselves. There was no head teacher as such; instead, the running of the school was by a col-

---

* *Frei* should not be construed as 'free' in the sense of license in matters of Waldorf education principles.

lege of teachers as a governing body, with various committees in support, the whole teaching staff being responsible for the day to day running of the school. This pattern of administration has for the most part survived.

It is impossible to describe the whole curriculum, pedagogy and didactics of a typical Waldorf/Steiner school in a few paragraphs, so that only the basic principles can be indicated here.[16] As might be expected, education is seen as a continuation of the incarnating process of the child as a spiritual being; the task of the teacher is to remove obstacles from the path of socialization, development and maturation of each one. Every child is not only incarnating, it is *re*-incarnating, and this knowledge helps to impart the necessary attitudes of respect, love and devotion, not to mention those of care, consideration and patience. Application and commitment to the task is taken for granted, as is the capacity for hard work. Waldorf teachers should never be tired — at least in the classroom, for Steiner, himself indefatigable, cheerily called upon all staff to reserve tiredness for some other occasion! It is a vocation demanding the highest possible personal and moral standards and qualities, and the willingness to take on commensurate responsibilities. In this respect, the meditation he gave for teachers of all Waldorf schools is worth quoting, for it contains the purest essence of Steiner education:

> Imbue thyself with the power of imagination;
> Have courage for the truth;
> Sharpen thy feeling for responsibility of soul.[17]

The three seven-year periods corresponding to infancy, childhood and adolescence provide the framework for progressive stages of education. In the life of a human infant the first period is one of devotion to its environment with *religious* zeal and application. Trust in whatever learning is absorbed presupposes the willingness to believe, and belief can be the stepping-stone to understanding and truth. This procedure is entirely appropriate and applicable to the character of this period. The element of willing associated with this first phase manifests as

The first Waldorf School in Stuttgart.

the will to knowledge, and Steiner responded to this by embarking on this lecturing activities and writing basic books on spiritual science. The second phase, that of childhood proper, recourse is made to *artistic* and creative activities of all kinds. These necessarily involve aesthetic principles, entailing the factors of feeling and beauty. The third period is when attention is paid to matters more to do with the outer world, in which *scientific* knowledge and practical skills are in demand. Factual knowledge is by very definition *true*; when facts are properly interpreted and applied, cleverness becomes wisdom. The fulfilment of the religious life is seen in Goodness, that of artistic activity in Beauty, and the goal of all scientific endeavour is Truth. Steiner always strove to combine these three 'eternal verities' in practice — a genuinely holistic approach. The following table may be helpful in making matters clear:

Period	Developmental mode	Cultural orientation	Attribute
1—7	Willing	Religion	Goodness
7–14	Feeling	Art	Beauty
14–21	Thinking	Science	Truth

The main principle of learning in children from birth to the time of shedding the so-called 'milk teeth' is that of *imitation.* The infant's whole environment is uncritically 'taken in,' for its intellectual powers are completely dormant; it is entirely open in its every attitude, utterly devoted to its immediate family and significant others, copying habits, gestures, accent and speech intonation — its whole vocation is indeed imitation. Education at this time is by exercise of the *will*; that is to say, by *action,* for what the infant sees being *done* it tries to do itself: there is no other way. The appropriate mode for its socialization and education obviously lies in providing surroundings and activities that are worthy of being imitated, for the foundations of the whole of the child's life are laid down during this period.

This places enormous responsibilities on parents, carers, minders, and kindergarten or nursery school 'teachers.' The child spends the whole of this first period in making its inherited body *its own*; and the indication that this process has been completed is the shedding of the milk teeth. The forces it hitherto deployed in building up its own physical/bodily organism are now free to serve the soul-spiritual, manifesting in its increased powers of memory, and by implication, its thinking. The child, now in approximately its seventh year, is maturationally ripe for attending school only at this time.

The stage of childhood proper — from the age of seven to the onset of puberty at around fourteen — is one of emphasis on what people around the child *say* rather than what they *do.* Children by very nature at this time display considerable powers of imagination and creativity, curiosity and interest in everything, all characterized by energy and enthusiasm. They are still very much bound up with their surroundings; they view the world subjectively rather than objectively, and behave accordingly. Their *feelings* should therefore be addressed in everything teachers do with their pupils. They are incapable of thinking entirely objectively, because their thinking is too subjective and admixed with feeling. All these behavioural attributes lend themselves very effectively to the educational strategy best adopted at this stage, and that is one based squarely on *authority.* Children need to be under its sway, and long for it, even if they do not seem to show this.

Inexperienced in the ways of the world, children are ever seeking wise and firm guidance from grown-ups, backed by an equally firm show of kind authority, which delineates, limits and establishes definite frames of reference. Such authority should arise as a perfectly natural practice adopted by adults and accepted by children, and this if properly administered results in contented children and unstressed adults. The methodology of teaching appropriate to this period is one that is thoroughly *artistic* in approach and operation. This does not mean, as many people think, that plenty of teaching of art as a subject is sufficient. Pupils of this age are naturally creative and imaginative, and these attributes should be taken up by the teacher, who should thoroughly rework and present all teaching material to them in ways that are artistic through and through, and refrain from offering it in conceptual terms; that is to say, by appealing to their — as yet immature — intellectual powers. The time for that is after puberty.

The attainment of sexual maturity marks the beginning of the stage when the intellect, with all it powers of analysis and objective *thinking,* is fully accessible. With these come attendant capacities for critical appraisal and fully objective judgement, as well as enhanced feelings of self and self-importance. Hitherto selfishness and self-interest have not been exercised in full consciousness; now it can be, and this involves strong and definite urges in the direction of *freedom.* Adolescents are properly associated with rebelliousness and wilfulness, for they see the world in a fresh light, and usually want to change it. Now is the time for their being taught in ways logical and systematic, for the most that any teacher can do at this stage is to provide the necessary facilities and guidance for *self*-education to take place. Young people are now perfectly capable of taking their own way forward and making their mark on the world, and this is what they should be allowed to do.

Science and religion

The emphasis on disseminating spiritual-scientific knowledge with special reference to the existing scientific disciplines continued during the early 1920s. In December 1919 Steiner gave a course on Light, and in March 1920 one on Heat; this was followed by twenty lectures to medical practitioners and students. The educational impulse continued, with lectures to teachers in Basel and Stuttgart, all the while making regular visits to the newly established Waldorf School there. To his great joy and satisfaction he was able to open the School for Spiritual Science at the Goetheanum during Michaelmas 1920.

In 1921 he was asked by a group of young Christian theologians whether he could help them in their wish for religious renewal. He agreed, whilst making it abundantly clear that he would be addressing them as a spiritual investigator and not as anyone committed to any religious establishment. This course laid the foundation for the Movement for Religious Renewal

Friedrich Rittelmeyer.

initiated the following year, which led on to the establishment of The Christian Community. A Protestant pastor, Dr Friedrich Rittelmeyer, became its leader, and further courses on theoretical, practical and pastoral theology followed in 1922 and 1924.[18]

Medicine for the whole person

As early as the turn of the century, Steiner had revealed his interest in medical matters in an article entitled 'Goethe and Medicine,' and as his investigative work into the human being proceeded, he was able to give advice on an *ad hoc* basis. In 1906, at the invitation of Dr Ludwig Noll, he gave a lecture on nutrition and curative methods, and in 1911 a course entitled *An*

*Dr Ita
Wegman*

Occult Physiology. Interest continued to grow, and in 1920 he delivered a course of twenty lectures for doctors and medical students in which he dealt with various aspects of human anatomy, physiology and pathology, as well as diagnosis, appropriate remedies and so on.

In each of the years 1921–24 Steiner gave further courses on medicine, indicating certain preparations for pharmaceutical products. These were subsequently developed in laboratories adjacent to the clinic set up at nearby Arlesheim, and at Stuttgart, and marketed under the name Weleda, now well-known throughout the world. Notable in this connection is Steiner's collaboration with a Dutch medical doctor, Ita Wegman, in writing *The Fundamentals of Therapy,* which appeared in 1924.

According to anthroposophical spiritual science, the human being is an extremely complex organism which, from different perspectives, may be seen as possessing not only a threefold, but also a fourfold, sevenfold and even a ninefold, nature (see *Theosophy,* Chapter 1). In many respects the most useful of these is the fourfold description of human nature, comprising physical body, etheric body, astral body and ego. These four vehicles should work in harmony with one another. In basic terms it is when they are *not* at ease with each other, not well integrated, that dis-ease arises.

Through our physical-material body, we maintain a connection with the inorganic world, itself lifeless. By ingesting food, the physical body brings the substances of the mineral world into mixture, form and dissolution by the same laws that are at work in the mineral world itself.

Scientific materialism designates the physical body as being the one and only constituent of the human being. Spiritual science, however, recognizes a further essential human principle in close formative relationship with the body: Steiner usually referred to it as the 'etheric body,' though he sometimes called it the 'life-body' or 'formative-forces-body' *(Bildekräfteleib),* pointing out that the term 'etheric' has nothing to do with the hypothetical ether of outdated physics. Etheric forces are manifested in the essential differences between the organic and the inorganic; an *organism* necessarily possesses an etheric body.

The etheric principle forms the basis for all formative life: it organizes the matter of the mineral world and shapes it to specific purposes according to genus and species of all living creation — plants, animals and human beings. A living structure does not receive its physical shape or form from anything else but the etheric conformation peculiar to it, which as an anabolic principle maintains the whole by means of regeneration. When damage or disease in an organism has reached the point where the life-processes of the requisite etheric body can no longer be maintained, it disintegrates — that is, it is given over to physical forces only — and death ensues. The body of a human being becomes a corpse directly etheric forces cease to be active in it.

Hence the individual etheric body in every person, as in every kind of animal and plant, is the agent of preserving the shape, form and function of all the bodily organs, which remain in spite of the continuous renewal of the matter which constitutes them. Other characteristics of etheric forces are the rhythmical repetition in shape and form of living entities, for example, the fronds of a fern, the petals of a flower, breathing, blood circulation, and so on. The human etheric body, however, differs from that of animals and plants, in that it is organized also to serve the purposes of the thinking spirit in the function of ideation and the powers of memory.

The third member of the human being is the so-called 'astral body' or 'sentient body.' The latter term, being more descriptive, is in many ways to be preferred, but the somewhat unfortunate term 'astral body,' often used indeterminately by quasi-'occultists' and spiritualists, persists in anthroposophical circles, thus generating confusion and misunderstanding.

The hallmark of the astral principle is *consciousness*. It is essentially a vehicle of pain and pleasure, sympathy and antipathy, likes and dislikes, impulse, craving and passions of all

Painting therapy.

kinds, all of which are absent in minerals and plants, which consist of physical and etheric principles only. In short, every creature which responds to external stimuli with *feeling* — and this means animals as well as humans — possesses an astral body.

The essential difference between animals and humans is that human beings possess a fourth member: the 'ego' or 'I.' The animal, by virtue of possessing an astral body, experiences consciousness. The human, by reason of possessing an ego, experiences *self*-consciousness. The ego represents individuality, that which guarantees the uniqueness of every man, woman and child. The special task of the ego is to purify and ennoble the other three members: it refines our wishes and desires through its influence on the astral body, establishes our habits, temperament and memory through its influence on the etheric body, and leaves its impression on the whole appearance and physiognomy, gestures and movements of the physical body.

It can be seen that this fourfold description (ego, astral body, etheric body, physical body) represents a more subtle differentiation than conventional 'body and soul' dualism. An older religious tradition acknowledged a threefold distinction between 'body, soul and spirit' and it is possible to relate this closely to the account given by spiritual science.

Anthroposophical medicine represents an extension of conventional medicine rather than an alternative to it. General medical practitioners who have undergone anthroposophical training therefore have a richer and more complex model of the human being than their conventional colleagues. They take into account symptoms of maladjustment among the four principles described above, symptoms which may have their origin not merely in physical pathology but in a whole range of aspects of both physical and spiritual wellbeing.

Anthroposophical medicine now has a long record of providing a truly holistic clinical approach. Therapy centres staffed by fully qualified doctors and nurses, with their ancillary helpers skilled, for example, in curative eurythmy, artistic therapy, rhythmical massage or biographical counselling, are being established in increasing numbers. Anthroposophical doctors have the advantage of being able to prescribe a wider range of treatments and medicines, all of which is beneficial to the patient. The anthroposophical pharmacopeia is widely recognized by medical authorities in Europe and elsewhere.

Triumphs and disasters

During the years 1922 and 1923 Steiner experienced in great measure both triumph and disaster — and treated 'those two impostors just the same.' He held lecture courses in many parts of Europe, fostering the interest that had been aroused by the practical application of anthroposophy in so many and diverse ways. He was especially in demand to speak about education, and his visits to England to lecture on educational and other topics at summer schools in 1922 (Oxford), 1923 (Ilkley) and again in 1924 (Torquay) were particularly happy occasions for him.

The West-East Congress in Vienna at which he attracted huge audiences was a great success and did much to spread his fame, but it was a very mixed year in terms of advancement. During these years he met with increasing opposition from political activists and other trouble-makers, who were not averse to resorting to physical as well as verbal abuse. Ominous rumblings of discontent were heard in the ranks of the younger anthroposophists, who considered that the older members were too fixed in their ways and their views. Steiner gave the so-called *Youth Course* in October 1922 in which he characterized the 'generation gap' as two groups who 'spoke an entirely different soul language,' thereby implying that the time had come for ego to confront ego squarely with mutual respect and regard, and that 'ethical individualism' was necessary for future progress. Further disaster was marked by the destruction by arson of the first Goetheanum on New Year's Eve 1922, as already mentioned.

The wide range of activities, and the many individuals to whom Rudolf Steiner lectured and with whom he worked during these

The ruins of the Goetheanum after the fire of New Year 1922/23.

postwar years, brought their own problems. The younger members, many of them coming to Dornach full of enthusiasm and zeal straight from university, college or other training, could not match the experience of many of the older members, and dissensions arose. Indeed, many researchers and collaborators were more intent on developing their own interests rather than those of spiritual science and its advancement. Rudolf Steiner's earnest wish was that the School of Spiritual Science should be a true *universitas* in that it should represent a 'whole' (in the modern sense of holistic), and that all disciplines should be fully cooperative.

However, around 1919 he observed that the work of the Society did not seem able to proceed in an integrated fashion; that to a great extent the work of 'various friends' at the Goetheanum proceeded 'side by side' with anthroposophical spiritual science rather than *from within it*. That members of the

Society did not seem to realize that the interests of anthroposophy should take precedence over selfish ambition was a source of great sorrow and vexation to Steiner, to whom it became clear that such lack of cohesion could only lead to disaster, and he was obliged to do some very straight talking indeed.[19] Sensing trouble ahead, he indicated before his death that Albert Steffen, the well-known Swiss poet and dramatist, should succeed him as President. Thereafter, in the absence of Steiner as authoritative source of guidance and advice, Steffen was

Albert Steffen.

faced with the unenviable task of preserving cohesion and sustaining morale in Dornach. This he continued to do, despite various crises, until his death in 1963.

When the General Anthroposophical Society was first formed in 1913 Rudolf Steiner did not actually become a member; instead he saw his role rather as a counsellor and guide. However, by early 1923 matters had reached crisis point, and he made the very painful and difficult decision to sanction the formation of a 'Free Anthroposophical Society' alongside the existing Society. This splinter organization, intended to cater for the younger members, was formed in Stuttgart on February 28, 1923. During the remainder of the year he worked on plans for restructuring the General Anthroposophical Society. In his opening address to the delegates at the Christmas Conference on December 24 he referred to these matters, going on to say: '... I can continue to lead the Anthroposophical Movement within the Anthroposophical Society only on the proviso that I myself take over the Presidency of the Anthroposophical Society which is to be founded anew here at the Goetheanum.'

On the morning of Christmas Day 1923 this came about with the laying of a 'spiritual foundation stone.' Steiner said: 'The ground in which the [foundation stone] was laid could be only in the hearts and souls of the persons united in the Society.' It was an event of the greatest possible importance and significance in the life of Rudolf Steiner. Anthroposophy had come of age, and was now fully incarnated in the world.

5. The final years

The second Goetheanum

Rudolf Steiner became ill on January 1, 1924, but despite the potential seriousness of this, he carried on work as usual. He lectured with urgent intensity, delivering talks to as many as five different audiences on as many subjects in a single day. Of particular importance were the eight courses on karma, penetrating in their depth and range of content. He gave courses on medical themes, tone eurythmy, education, agriculture, speech

The second Goetheanum.

production and dramatic art. He gave lectures to theologians interested in religious renewal, as well as talks on a wide range of topics to the workers on the second Goetheanum. But the strain induced by years of worry and overwork, together with his illness, was now taking its toll. With the greatest sorrow and reluctance, he decided that the lecture delivered on September 28 must be his last.

However, he continued to occupy himself with the second Goetheanum, which was begun in 1925. As in the case of the first Goetheanum, he chose to make a scale model rather than draw up plans on paper. He had pondered for a year before deciding on its form and construction, realizing that it must be much bigger than the first, and include laboratories, special lecture rooms, studios and workshops. However, he got no further than modelling the exterior shell. He told a close friend that the new Goetheanum would be paid for by the money paid out by the insurance companies. 'They will hate to pay us,' he said. 'It will no longer be money given with love, and I must use it accordingly. The new Goetheanum will be built not of wood but of a dead material — concrete.' But to all who see this huge building with its sculpted lines resting atop the hill in Dornach, it is unforgettable. Nestling among the foothills of the Jura Mountains, it seems as ageless as they are — as if it has always been there.

The birth of biodynamic farming

In 1924 two important new initiatives were realized. During 1921 and 1922 Steiner's indications for research work at the biological research laboratory at the Goetheanum had reached certain conclusions. A number of farmers and growers approached him for advice on problems relating to poor soil fertility, degenerate seed-strains and the spread of animal disease. From then on, he was repeatedly invited to give practical advice to farmers and horticulturists. The outcome was a course of eight lectures in June 1924 which heralded the development of what has become known worldwide as 'biodynamic agriculture.'

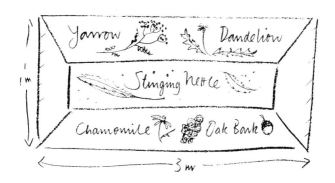

Plan of a biodynamic compost heap and its preparations.

Steiner deeply deplored the use of chemical fertilizers for the reason that *dead* materials were being introduced into what was a *living* organism — the earth — into which should be applied only life-endowed substances. Already in 1923, specific biodynamic compost and spray preparations were made for the first time on Steiner's direct instructions. He held that each farm is an organic individuality, and should be as self-sufficient as possible, pointing out that disease in both animals and plants become rampant in conditions of mono-culture and frequent buying-in of livestock and fodder. Steiner was a true ecologist, and brought to agriculture and horticulture a genuinely holistic approach, arguing that plants germinate, grow and fruit as products dependent on sun, earth, air and water, and that therefore the whole universe is engaged. Biodynamic methods incorporate fundamental principles and practices which mark them as not merely an extension of ordinary organic methods, and the two should not be confused. The biodynamic movement was the first to develop a certified marketing label — Demeter — which assures consumers of the authenticity of biodynamic products.

Rudolf Steiner in 1923.

The founders of curative education. Werner Pache, Franz Löffler, Ita Wegman, Siegfried Pickert, Albert Strohschein.

Children in need of special care

Early in 1923 three young students who were working with mentally handicapped children approached Steiner for advice, which resulted in his giving a course of twelve lectures on Curative Education in the summer, and prompted the opening of a home at nearby Arlesheim, directed by Dr Wegman. The initiative soon spread, resulting in the foundation in Europe and the rest of the world of hundreds of establishments set up for mentally retarded children and young people 'in need of special care.' Notable among these are those of the Camphill Movement, although there are also many other similar establishments of varying sizes in many countries.

Last days

In spite of rapidly failing health, Steiner made no effort to spare himself. He delivered his last lecture at Dornach on September 28. He asked for his bed to be moved into the studio which contained the enormous statue of the Representative of Man, referred to earlier (see p. 47). As long as he was able, he worked on the carving, but even when his condition became so grave as to confine him entirely to his bed he carried on writing, reading, and attending to correspondence. He continued with the weekly instalments of his autobiography *The Course of My Life,* and *Letters to Members,** discussing medical questions with his physician and collaborator Dr Ita Wegman, and holding discussions with Dr Guenther Wachsmuth concerning Society matters. Wracked with pain, he gradually became weaker and more emaciated, yet he drove himself relentlessly and uncomplainingly on despite advice urging him to conserve what little strength he still had ...

At the foot of each instalment of his biography Rudolf Steiner habitually wrote 'To be continued.' The one which he handed out shortly before he died bore no such message. On March 30, 1925, in full consciousness of both spiritual and material worlds, he folded his hands over his breast, closed his eyes, and drew his final breath.

---

* Published in English as *Anthroposophical Leading Thoughts.*

6. A continuing story

A champion of freedom

Steiner was not in any sense a 'master' or 'guru,' and did not regard members of the anthroposophical movement in any way as 'followers,' but always as free agents. In his book *Theosophy* he wrote:

> The spiritual researcher approaches his student with the injunction: You are not required to believe what I tell you but to think it, to make it the content of your own thought world; then my thoughts will of themselves bring about the recognition of their truth.'[20]

That some of his lectures and books appear to be 'difficult' is not a fault to be laid against them. It requires a certain courage, as well as the capacity for making the necessary effort, to take up new ideas, accept unorthodox premises, and incorporate them into one's whole world-view. Steiner always refused to 'popularize' his ideas, or — which would be very easy in some cases — to make sensational pronouncements merely for the sake of drawing attention to anthroposophy in the hope of making converts. Ever a believer in the freedom of the individual, he left people to make up their own minds about things, and take their own decisions.

As originator of the philosophy of 'ethical individualism,' he identified himself as a champion of freedom at the individual level and of liberty at the societal level. The General Anthroposophical Society is an entirely public institution, and not in any way 'secret,' exclusive or doctrinaire, and this is true also of affiliated organizations. Membership does not impose duties, as these are voluntarily assumed, and is open 'without distinction of nationality, social standing, religion, scientific or artistic conviction, to any person who considers the existence of such an institution as the Goetheanum, the School of Spiritual Science, to be justified.'

Seventy years on

It is only with the passage of time that his work has come more and more to be recognized, and Steiner anticipated this. He was alert to the likelihood that his message and its significance would not be understood, and would be met with lack of interest and even hostility; and events bore this out. He was also aware that his philosophies and their practical application would take time to become established, and would grow only slowly; but this was what he wished. He knew that *pragmatism,*

Biodynamic produce in the supermarket.

A Waldorf kindergarten at Raphael House Waldorf School, Wellington, New Zealand.

understood in its true sense of making practical consequences the test of truths, would eventually be seen to be on his side; that time tells every tale. This has proved to be so, for there is not a single area in which spiritual-scientific principles took firm root which has not experienced growth and development.

Since Rudolf Steiner's death, the application of anthroposophical spiritual science in several areas of practical life has developed steadily. It is now possible to purchase produce from biodynamic farms and gardens from supermarkets and health-shops all over Europe, America and the New World. The worldwide Waldorf schools movement is now represented by well over six hundred schools, with more opening at the rate of one hundred or so per year. In many countries, the demand for education along Waldorf lines greatly exceeds the supply, and dozens of kindergartens and schools have waiting lists. Home schools for 'children in need of special care' have likewise increased, as have the residential establishments and village communities which strive to achieve self-sufficiency through

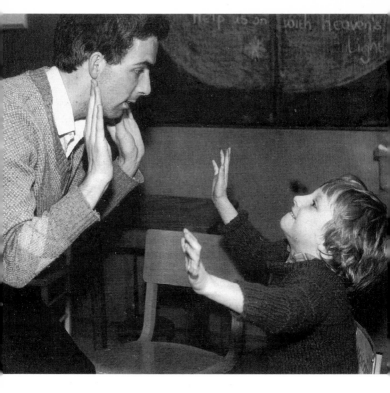

Curative education. A rhythmic co-ordination exercise.

agriculture, craftwork and other activities. In medicine, widespread public concern over certain aspects of conventional medicine and a desire for 'safe' alternatives to drugs, has led to growing interest in the well-established centres of practice of anthroposophical medicine, in some cases within the framework of public or National Health Service facilities.

A truly holistic science

Steiner maintained that where spiritual science was concerned, theory and practice coincide. It follows that the application of ideas and concepts based on incomplete understanding of the *symptoms* or *phenomena* — as is necessarily the case with materialist methodologies — is likely to result in longer-term problems. The increasingly calamitous trends that are evident in the areas of economics, agriculture, education and the social services, provide good examples of this lack of deeper understanding in modern times.

Unfortunately, materialism has secured a very firm grip on western-type culture, and the price still has to be paid for this one-sided attitude. The modern tendency of scientists — and that includes sociologists, economists and educational researchers — towards *reductionism* has resulted in unbalanced thinking; though this is already eliciting opposition from growing numbers who see the wisdom of adopting a *holistic* perspective. The idea of a 'universal' rather than 'specialist' perspective is returning, in recognition of the limitations of narrow fragmentalism.

In terms of relationship to their work, the differences in fundamental attitude between a conventional engineer, technician, or anyone else employed in modern technology, and someone running a biodynamic farm, teaching in a Steiner school, or practising as an anthroposophical general practitioner, are bound to be considerable. In the case of the former, it need not matter at all what kind of world-view they have; but where the latter are concerned it matters a very great deal. Once having embraced a philosophy that envisages a world in which every natural process is seen to be an outcome of spirit at work in matter, reversion to any kind of materialistic *Weltanschauung* ('world-view') is most unlikely. Steiner maintained that the spiritual sources of religion, art and science (in the sense of knowledge or wisdom) were the same. He pointed out that these three important fields of human culture and endeavour were closely related during our early history, and that they had gradually become separate activities, but would, in the course of human history, become reunited.

The multi-disciplinary nature of his own researches and activities bears witness to these observations. It was his earnest wish and endeavour to steer the sciences out of their highly specialized, fragmented approach towards a new, comprehensive view of nature in which spiritual reality takes its proper place. The wide range and diversity of themes that Steiner covered, apparently with such mastery and ease, was a constant source of amazement to those who knew him. But those close to him knew that he was thorough in his ways, energetic and hard-working, with all the qualities of a scholar in the best sense of the word. His investigations into the spiritual realms pre-supposed these attributes; for far from finding access to them easy, the tasks involved in the acquiring of 'facts' in the ordinary sense were far from straightforward, requiring patience and tenacity.

A peculiarity of spiritual science is that it is often extraordinarily difficult to *memorize,* to hold concepts concerning it firmly in the mind. As the subject-matter is, by its very nature, not representative of objects and events of the sensory world to which we are all accustomed, it is not surprising that newcomers to anthroposophy find its study very demanding, at least to start with. A cursory reading of his books or reported lectures is impossible; it is invariably necessary to study them, and moreover, to make their contents one's own. Relying on memory alone is insufficient, for it is always necessary for proper understanding to think their contents through, reflectively and meditatively. This is a creative process, involving patient and often persistent effort and repeated application to the task; but the knowledge and insights gained as a result are often of great benefit. Above all, the most valuable conclusion reached by every serious student of spiritual science is that it *works.*

References

1. Steiner, R. *The Course of My Life,* p.174.
2. Steiner, R. *The Course of My Life,* p.71.
3. Steiner, R. *The Course of my Life,* p.237.
4. Steiner, R. *The Course of my Life,* p.299.
5. Steiner, R. *The Course of my Life,* p.301.
6. Steiner, R. *Anthroposophical Leading Thoughts* (letter of November 16, 1924).
7. Wachsmuth, G. *The Life and Work of Rudolf Steiner,* Whittier Books, 1955.
8. Wachsmuth, G. *The Life and Work of Rudolf Steiner,* p.128.
9. Landau, R. *God is My Adventure,* pp.95ff and 349ff. Ivor Nicholson & Watson, 1935.
10. Landau, R. *God is my Adventure,* p.128..
11. Childs, G.J. *Steiner Education in Theory and Practice,* pp.35ff. Floris Books, Edinburgh 1991.
12. Steiner, R. *Towards Social Renewal.*
13. Wachsmuth, G. *The Life and Work of Rudolf Steiner,* p.358.
14. Steiner, R. Lecture, Stuttgart, June 22, 1919.
15. Steiner, R. *Study of Man,* p.15.
16. Rudolf Steiner gave many lecture courses on education, some of which presuppose knowledge of basic spiritual science. For main titles, see Further Reading.
17. Steiner, R. *Study of Man,* p.190.
18. Rittelmeyer, F. *Rudolf Steiner Enters My Life,* Floris Books, 1982.
19. Steiner, R. Lecture, Stuttgart, January 23, 1923.
20. Steiner, R. *Theosophy,* p.225.

Photographic acknowledgments

Hulton Deutsch 13; Paul Bock 84; Fiona Christellar 83; Verlag am Goetheanum 6, 9, 10, 11, 14, 18, 20, 21, 23, 27, 33, 36, 38, 39, 41, 42, 45, 46, 47, 49, 56, 59, 67, 72, 73, 78, 79; Michiel Wijnbergh 82

Further reading

The following are considered Steiner's basic books:
(The volume number of Steiner's collected works, the German *Gesamtausgabe,* is shown in brackets)

The Philosophy of Spiritual Activity also known as *The Philosophy of Freedom,* Steiner Press, London 1964. New translation published as *Intuitive Thinking as a Spiritual Path: A Philosophy of Freedom,* Anthroposophic Press, New York 1995 (Vol. 4).

Theosophy: An Introduction to the Spiritual Processes in Human Life and the Cosmos, Anthroposophic Press, New York 1994 (Vol. 9).

How to Know Higher Worlds: A Modern Path of Initiation, Anthroposophic Press, New York 1994. (Formerly published as *Knowledge of the Higher Worlds and its Attainment)* (Vol. 10).

Occult Science: An Outline, Steiner Press, London 1979. Also published as *An Outline of Occult Science,* Anthroposophic Press, New York 1972 (Vol. 13).

Christianity as Mystical Fact and the Mysteries of Antiquity, Steiner Press, London 1972 (Vol. 8).

The Course of my Life, Anthroposophic Press, New York, 1951, 1986. Also published as *Rudolf Steiner, An Autobiography,* Steinerbooks, New York 1977 (Vol. 28).

Truth and Knowledge or *Truth and Science,* Steinerbooks, New York 1981 (Vol. 3).

The Spiritual Guidance of the Individual and Humanity, Anthroposophic Press, New York 1992 (Vol. 15).

The Redemption of Thinking, Anthroposophic Press, New York 1983 (Vol. 74).

The Theory of Knowledge Implicit in Goethe's World-Conception. Now published as *The Science of Knowing,* Mercury Press, New York 1988 (Vol. 2).

Four Mystery Plays, Steiner Press, London 1982 (Vol. 14).

Towards Social Renewal, Steiner Press, London 1977 (Vol. 23).

Anthroposophical Leading Thoughts, Steiner Press, London 1987 (Vol. 26).

Fundamentals of Therapy, by Rudolf Steiner and Ita Wegman, Steiner Press, London 1983 (Vol. 27).

The following lecture cycles presume a basic knowledge of Steiner's terminology developed in the above basic books:

The Gospel of St John, Anthroposophic Press, New York 1984 (Vol.104).

The Gospel of St Luke, Steiner Press, London 1968 (Vol. 114).

The Gospel of St Mark, Steiner Press, London and Anthroposophic Press, New York 1986 (Vol. 139).

The Gospel of St Matthew, Steiner Press, London and Anthroposophic Press, New York 1986 (Vol. 123).

The Gospel of St John and Its Relation to the Other Three Gospels, particularly to the Gospel of St Luke, Anthroposophic Press, New York 1982 (Vol. 112).

The Apocalypse of St John: Lectures on the Book of Revelation, Steiner Press, London 1985 (Vol. 104).

From Jesus to Christ, Steiner Press, Sussex 1991 (Vol. 131).

From Buddha to Christ, Anthroposophic Press, New York 1978.

The Fifth Gospel, Steiner Press, London 1985 (Vol. 148).

An Occult Physiology, Steiner Press, London 1983 (Vol. 128).

The following lectures are on education:

The Education of the Child in the Light of Anthroposophy, Steiner Press, London, and Anthroposophic Press, New York 1981.

Foundations of Human Experience, Anthroposophic Press, New York 1996 (Previously published as *The Study of Man)* (Vol. 293).

Practical Advice to Teachers, Steiner Press, London 1988 (Vol. 294).

Discussions with Teachers, Steiner Press, Bristol 1992 (Vol. 295).

A Modern Art of Education, Steiner Press, London 1981 (Vol. 307).

The Kingdom of Childhood, Anthroposophic Press, New York 1995 (Vol. 311).

Waldorf Education and Anthroposophy, Vol I. Anthroposophic Press, New York 1995 (Vol. 304).

Genius of Language, Anthroposophic Press, New York 1995 (Vol. 299).

General biographies/introductions

Barfield, Owen *Saving the Appearances: A Study in Idolatry.*

Lissau, Rudi, *Rudolf Steiner, Life, Work, Inner Path and Social Initiatives,* Hawthorn Press, Stroud 1987.

Rittelmeyer, Friedrich *Rudolf Steiner Enters My Life,* Floris Books, Edinburgh 1982.

Shepherd, A.P. *Scientist of the Invisible,* Floris Books, Edinburgh 1991.

Wachsmuth, Guenther, *The Life and Work of Rudolf Steiner,* Garber, 1989.

A Man Before Others: Rudolf Steiner Remembered, Steiner Press, Bristol, 1993.

Religious/philosophical

Bock, Emil *The Apocalypse of St John,* Floris Books, Edinburgh 1986.

—, *St Paul,* Floris Books, Edinburgh 1993.

—, *The Three Years: the Life of Christ between Baptism and Ascension,* Floris Books, Edinburgh 1987.

Frieling, Rudolf *Christianity and Islam: a Battle for the True Image of Man,* Floris Books, Edinburgh 1980.

—, *Christianity and Reincarnation,* Floris Books, Edinburgh 1977.

Hindes, James, *Renewing Christianity,* Floris Books, Edinburgh 1995 and Anthroposophic Press, New York 1996.

Prokofieff, Sergei O. *Eternal Individuality,* Temple Lodge, London 1992.

—, *The Spiritual Origins of Eastern Europe and the Future Mysteries of the Holy Grail,* Temple Lodge, London 1993.

Welburn, Andrew *The Beginnings of Christianity,* Floris Books, Edinburgh 1991.

Education

Calgren, Frans, *Education Towards Freedom,* Lanthorn Press, 1993.

Childs, Gilbert, *Steiner Education,* Floris Books, Edinburgh 1995.

Harwood, A.C., *The Way of a Child,* Steiner Press, London 1979.

Murphy, C, *Emil Molt,* Floris Books, Edinburgh 1991.

König, Karl, *Brothers and Sisters,* Floris Books, Edinburgh 1993.

Special education

Clarke, P., H. Kofsky, J. Laurel, *To a Different Drumbeat,* Hawthorn Press, Stroud 1989.

Hansmann, Henning, *Education for Special Needs,* Floris Books, Edinburgh 1992.

Luxford, Michael, *Children with Special Needs,* Floris Books, Edinburgh and Anthroposophic Press, New York 1994.

Pietzner, Cornelius (ed.), *Candle on the Hill,* Floris Books, Edinburgh and Anthroposophic Press, New York 1990.

Weihs, Thomas, *Children in Need of Special Care,* Souvenir Press.

Biodynamics

Koepf, H, Bo Pettersen and W Schaumann, *Bio-dynamic Agriculture, an Introduction.* Anthroposophic Press, New York 1976.

Schilthuis, *Biodynamic Agriculture,* Floris Books, Edinburgh and Anthroposophic Press, New York 1994.

Artistic impulses

Bayes, Kenneth, *Living Architecture,* Floris Books, Edinburgh and Anthroposophic Press, New York 1994.

Useful addresses

In the UK:

The Anthroposophical Society in Great Britain
Rudolf Steiner House
35 Park Road
London NW1 6XT

The Steiner Schools Fellowship
Kidbrooke Park
Forest Row, E. Sussex RH18 5JX

The Bio-Dynamic Agricultural Association
Woodman Lane, Clent
Stourbridge, W. Midlands DY9 9PX

Anthroposophical Medical Association
Rudolf Steiner House
(see above)

Weleda (UK) Ltd
Heanor Road
Ilkeston Derbyshire DE7 8DR

In the USA:
Anthroposophical Society in
    America
529 West Grant Place
Chicago, IL 60614
(312) 248-5606

Anthroposophic Press Inc
RR 4, Box 94A1
Hudson, NY 12534
(518) 851-2054

Biodynamic Farming &
    Gardening Association
PO Box 550
Kimberton, PA 19442
(610) 935-7797

Association of Waldorf
    Schools of North America
3911 Bannister Road
Fair Oaks, CA 95628
(916) 961-0927

Weleda Inc
PO Box 249
Congers, NY 10920
(914)268-8572

Physicians Association for
    Anthroposophic Medicine
c/o Joan Takacs
5909 SE Division
Portland, OR 97206
(503) 234- 1531

Camphill Foundation
PO Box 290
Kimberton, PA 19442
(610) 935-0200

In Australia
Anthropsophical Society in
    Australia
20 Harris Road,
Dural NSW 2158

In Canada
Anthroposophical Society in
    Canada
81 Lawton Blvd, Toronto Ont
M4V 1Z6

In New Zealand
Anthroposophical Society in
New Zealand
c/o Brian Butler
21 Rimu Street, Taupo

South Africa
Anthroposophical Society in
Southern Africa
PO Box 65119, Benmore 2010

International
General Anthroposophical So-
ciety
Goetheanum, 4143 Dornach,
Switzerland

Index

Figures in italics refer to illustrations